Dedication

To all those teachers and catechists who can look into the

eyes of a child and see the light of Christ

shining there.

Come Holy Spirit

Holy Spirit, all caring, all loving God,
you know and love the children in my class.
You know how each one learns,
and what each needs most from me.
May the activities in this book guide me
as I try to reach and engage each child.
Inspire me to create my own activities, too,
and to rely on you for creative ways to make
every class I teach both interesting and fun.
Help me to remember and reach out to
the timid ones, the active ones,
the slow ones, the clever ones,
and the ones who need to
see, hear, touch, and say.
They require so much more than lectures
or reading from a textbook.
Give me a boost, please, dear Holy Spirit.
Help me to teach *every* child in my class
in precisely the way each needs to be taught.
Amen.

Gwen Costello

SCHOOL YEAR
activities

for
Religion
Classes

TWENTY-THIRD PUBLICATIONS
BAYARD ◉ Mystic, CT 06355

Twenty-Third Publications/Bayard
185 Willow Street
P.O. Box 180
Mystic, CT 06355
(860) 536-2611
(800) 321-0411

ISBN:1-58595-107-2
Library of Congress Catalog Card Number: 00-131568
Printed in the U.S.A.

Contents

School Year Activities for Religion Classes

Introduction

Children love activity and variety—even in religion class—especially in religion class. They like moving around and keeping busy. They like to see, hear, talk, taste, and touch. Some children can learn by listening to the teacher, and others can learn by reading the text, but most learn best by being more fully involved with the lesson, and are thus more apt to make it their own.

The activities in this book offer teachers and catechists a great variety of ways to involve children in their religion classes. Most take just five to ten minutes and all can be used to supplement almost any lesson. For convenience, the activities are ordered by the month, beginning in September with the first class of the year and ending in May, which includes activities that focus on both Mary and Pentecost. Seasons and feasts covered include: All Saints Day, Thanksgiving, Advent, Christmas, Epiphany, Lent, Valentine's Day, Easter, and Pentecost. For each month of the school year there are four or more activities, plus seven "all-year-long" activities at the back of the book.

My hope is that these suggested activities

 will inspire religion teachers to devise their own games, review techniques, creative activities, and ways to pray.

September Activities

Getting Acquainted

Try this activity with any age group. Write out a number of questions (one each for half the number of students in your class), and cut these into strips. Write out answers to these questions on separate strips. Fold the strips and place them in a bowl. Then invite all of the children to come forward to take a strip. After a moment of silence to study the question or answer, have class members begin searching for the person holding the matching question or answer. When the match has been made, ask pairs to share the following information:

My name is…

My favorite book is…

My favorite prayer is…

A place I like to pray is…

(Add any questions that might be more appropriate for your group.)

The questions and answers you use can also be ones based on what you will be covering in this lesson (for example, the Mass, sacraments, Scripture, prayer, God the Father, Jesus, the Holy Spirit, etc.).

Who's the Teacher?

Sometimes we are so concerned about learning the names of the children, we forget to tell the children who we are. Parents, of course, want to know the teacher's name, and it's amazing how often a child has to say "I don't know." To avoid this, prepare and duplicate for each child a hand-out sheet that contains the following: your name and phone number, the name and theme of your text, the date and time your class will meet, and any guidelines for parent participation you can offer. This might be the beginning of regular "parent notes" from you that contain information about activities you have scheduled, assignments you want completed, or family participation you require.

Learning Names Quickly

One of the most important things we catechists can do to start the year off right is to develop a good relationship with those we teach. This involves learning their names quickly, a sure sign that we are personally interested in them. You can do this by spending time in your first class playing two get-acquainted games. The first and easiest involves getting the entire class into a large circle. Begin by saying your name and your favorite Bible story. The child to your right must repeat your name and favorite story and then his or her own, and so it goes around the circle. The children love the challenge of struggling to remember all the names and stories, and the repetition will help you get names straight more quickly.

The second activity is an autograph game. Give the children (and yourself) a piece of paper with the words, "God loves..." at the top. Ask that everyone in the room get the autograph of every other person. However, before anyone gives an autograph, he or she must say, "My full name is _____, and God loves me." Then they can sign their names any way they want: full name, nickname, last name only, etc. This game is fun and it helps the entire class get acquainted.

They Are Special to God

At one of your first classes of the year explain to children that even though they may not be aware of it, God calls each of them by name. To highlight this, give them name tags and ask them to print their names on them in bright colors. Then invite them to stand in a circle with their name tags on.

Pray aloud for each child in this way: "Thank you, God, for calling _____ by name." Each time the entire group should repeat the prayer after you. When the last child in the circle has been prayed for, invite the children to step forward one by one so you can trace a cross on each forehead, saying, "_____, remember God's love for you."

This activity also has another purpose. It helps the children (and you) quickly learn one another's names.

Making the Rules Together

It is very important to have rules in religion class, whether your teaching space is large or small, in a classroom or a living room. Rules give children a sense of security because they know what is expected of them and what will happen if they break the rules.

Before you post any rules, however, invite the children to suggest the kinds of rules they think they need. Ask someone to jot them down as they are named. Then read each aloud and ask the children to trim the list to four rules. Almost always children come up with variations of the following:

•Never interrupt when someone else is talking (catechist or child)

•No loud talking or running (unless we're outside)

•Raise hands before speaking and wait to be called upon

•Show respect for everyone in the class

Once you decide on your class rules, explain that if a child breaks one of them, you will put a check beside his or her name. At the end of the class, children with checks must stay (very briefly) to talk to you. (Ask them to do better the next time, and then say this prayer with them: "Thank you, loving God, for _____. Help her/him to love and respect others. Amen." This is usually all you have to do. However, on those rare occasions when a child gets three or more checks, explain that you will be calling parents (and then do so).

All Together Now

A get-acquainted activity that children enjoy is creating a class bulletin board (or class poster). If available, use a Polaroid camera to take a photo of each child and arrange these on the bulletin board or poster. Invite the children to write their names under their photos. If a camera is not available, invite the children to draw a picture or symbol of themselves and attach these drawings to the bulletin board or poster—and again have them add their signatures. Together decide on a class motto, a class prayer, and a class patron saint and print these at the top.

A Student's Prayer

Make copies of the following prayer for each child in your class. Explain that this prayer can be for religion class as well as for their regular school activities. Pray it together as you begin or end your September classes.

Thank you, God, for this new school year. Help me to use

it well by doing my best. Open my mind to everything I am taught this year. May I give my teachers attention and respect. May I give my classmates courtesy and kindness. Please be with me as I study and as I play. Guide me in all that I do and in all that I say. Amen.

October Activities

Creative Ways to Pray

Ask your class: "How can we start and end our classes with more meaningful prayers?" After some discussion of this, suggest that they should take turns planning new and different opening and closing prayers for each class. (Those who forget to prepare can choose a formal prayer from the textbook.) Possible methods of prayer might be: a prayer procession for which everyone leaves the room and processes back carrying items for the class prayer table; prayer blessings for which the child opens wide his or her arms and prays that God will bless the class and help them as they try to learn about their faith; laying on of hands, as is done at the anointing of the sick. The leader can place his or her hands on each forehead and say, "God bless you." This can also be done with holy water by making a cross on each class member's forehead. After offering possible suggestions, allow children to be creative in devising their own prayers and methods of prayer.

Praying for Pets

On or near the feast of St. Francis of Assisi, invite the children in your class to write the names of their pets on small slips of paper. As they hold these slips, pray the following prayer to St. Francis.

Dear Saint Francis, you loved all creatures great and small. You praised and blessed the Lord for the animals who shared your life. Joining our prayer to yours, we too thank and praise God for our pets. We give you thanks, God, our Creator, for your wonderful and surprising gifts: for birds and fishes, and all creatures of the sea and sky, for wild animals and tame animals, for cats and dogs and for all our pets. Help us, God, our Creator, to take good care of our pets. Thank you for the happiness they give us. Saint Francis of Assisi, pray for us and pray for our pets too. Amen.

Planning Prayer Services

Involve those you teach in the planning of your prayer services. Invite them to write out topics that interest them and then place these in a container. Draw one topic out and let it become the theme for your service. The children take turns serving on the following "committees": Scripture, litany/prayer, rituals, and music.

Obviously the Scripture committee looks for verses that teach something about your theme. The litany/prayer committee composes requests, prayers of thanksgiving, lists of saints, etc., for group prayer, depending on your theme.

The rituals committee decides what prayerful action might best accompany your service, for example, blessings with water or oil, writing out something to be placed on your prayer table, "signing" a formal prayer, etc.

The music committee chooses the songs you will sing or the taped music you will listen to. They decide, too, when and if you will walk in procession.

In addition to these elements, always have at least two minutes of silent prayer as part of this experience. The children will learn a great deal about prayer forms in this way and they will be much more actively involved with your class prayer.

Relying on the Saints

October is a good time to reflect with children on our call to follow Jesus. In preparation for All Saint's Day (which is celebrated on November 1), invite children to think about their name saint (or a favorite saint) and to compose a prayer to that saint for someone who needs a boost (a lonely neighbor, an elderly relative, a child who feels left out). A sample prayer might be: "Saint Joseph, please pray for my neighbor Mrs. Carlyle. Ask Jesus to help her feel better. Amen." If possible give the children unlined index cards for these prayers and, if time permits, encourage them to decorate them.

Saint Sharing

To commemorate All Saints Day, why not launch a weekly saint-sharing session? First, ask for volunteers who are willing to prepare five-minute presentations about their favorite saints. Place the names of these volunteers in a special container. Each week draw one out and ask that person to be the presenter for the coming week. Encourage creative formats, for example: drawings, puppets, poetry, role-play, etc. Be sure to stick to the five-minute time frame.

A True Celebration

Since All Saints Day does not get the attention other holidays and church feasts do, try to celebrate it in a special way with your class. Prior to your class celebration, ask the children to answer in writing (with help from parents) the following:

What is your full name? Why were you given this name? Who is your patron saint? What interesting facts or stories do

you know about this saint? What can you bring to class that symbolizes your patron saint? (Sample items might be a flower, a small rock, a drawing, a holy card, etc.) For your actual celebration, invite the children to show the symbol they have chosen and to share with the class any information they may have about their patron saints. Conclude with a prayer litany, using all the name-saints, plus your own.

Writing Saint Prayers

Children get very frustrated with activities that seem to have no purpose. For example, drawing pictures that are never used again, assigning homework that is never checked, or doing an activity that seems to have no point in relation to the lesson. So really try to make use of any extra assignments you give the children. Here's a typical example.

Ask the children—with help from their parents—to write a

prayer to their name-saint. If they were not named for a saint, they could choose a favorite saint. In a note to parents, ask them to help their child learn something about the saint and to discuss together what should be in the prayer.

In the class before All Saints Day, hang a poster with every child's name on it in your prayer area. During your class prayer service, invite children one by one to stand near the poster as they pray their saint prayers. Then they should tape the prayers onto the poster near their name. Keep this poster up during the month of November and use the prayers several more times before the children take them home.

November Activities

How Good It Is!

Even if your textbook doesn't offer a specific lesson about the feast of All Saints (November 1st), share this activity with your class. Stress the "All" in the name because we not only honor all who are saints, but also all those in your class who are called to be saints. Many children have a notion of "saint" that is far removed from anything in their daily lives. Thus, invite them to discuss what it means to be a good person.

When you feel satisfied that they understand "good" to mean concern for others, for the world around them, and for family and friends, ask each child to list three good things he or she has recently done. These lists should be taped closed and placed in a box decorated with the words: How good it is to be a saint!

On the class nearest to the feast of All Saints, focus on the many good things each has done. Have each child make a name tag that includes the words: "I do good things." Then, carry your "good" box in procession (to background march-

ing music) to your class prayer table. There pray together in thanksgiving for all the good people in your lives.

If possible during the last ten minutes of class share and enjoy a special treat. How "good" it is to share!

Praying Our Thanks

During November help your class prepare for Thanksgiving by reminding them that every day is a good day for giving thanks to God. During your first class in November, begin with a Thanksgiving prayer service. First have the children write on small slips of paper one thing for which they are particularly grateful. They can hold these slips as they process to your prayer table while singing, "Now Thank We All Our God."

When you reach the prayer table, stand in a circle around it. Ask one of the children to read this short verse from 1 Thessalonians 5, 6: "Rejoice always, pray without ceasing and give thanks to God at every moment. This is the will of God; this is what you are called to as Christians." After the reading, begin a litany of thanksgiving by holding up your own slip of paper and say-ing: "For _____, I thank God." The children can respond, "Let us all thank God."

Each child in turn then reads what is on his or her slip.

After all have had a turn, place the slips in a container on your prayer table where they remain until Thanksgiving.

Special Thank-You Box

One way to focus on thanksgiving prayer around the time of Thanksgiving is to have a class "give thanks" box. Invite the children to write on slips of paper items for which they would like the entire class to give thanks. These should be substantial things like the recovery of a loved one, a good decision by someone in a leadership role, a scientific or medical discovery that benefits the poor, etc. In each class, draw out one or more items from this box and pray in thanksgiving as a class.

Thank-You Notes

To help children focus on the people around them who care for them and guide them, invite them to write a thank-you note to a parent, a special teacher, a scout leader, etc. These notes might have the following on the outside page: "God has given me many gifts. One of them is you." The children can print these words and then decorate the cards with flowers, hearts, or any appropriate designs. The important thing is that they recognize the "people" gifts that God has given them and say thanks for these.

Thanksgiving Proclamation

"Don't let a day go by without saying thanks." This is a message we should repeat often to the children in our religion classes until they know it by heart. As Thanksgiving draws near, include the following "Proclamation of Thanksgiving" as part of your third class in November.

Walk in procession to your class prayer table. One child carries the Bible, one carries a candle (unlit), and one carries a scroll. As you process, sing "We Thank You, We Do" (to the tune of Happy Birthday). When you reach the prayer table, gather in a circle around it, and the child with the candle places it on the table and lights it. The child with the Bible places it on the table (open to Philippians 4:4). The child with the scroll opens it and reads these words:

"I hereby appoint this day to be one of thanksgiving. Let us thank God for the many blessings we have received. May we never take them for granted. It has now been proclaimed; let us now see it through."

At this point, a pre-designated child should go to the prayer table, pick up the Bible and begin to read: "Rejoice in the Lord always; again I say rejoice. Let your gentleness be known to everyone. The Lord is near. Do not worry about anything, but in everything with words of thanksgiving let your prayers come before God. And the peace of God, which surpasses all understanding, will guard your hearts and your minds in Christ Jesus."

Following this reading, invite the children to offer spontaneous prayers of thanksgiving.

December Activities

Sending Notes Home

During the liturgical seasons: Advent, Christmas, Epiphany, Lent, Easter, Pentecost, send notes home to parents to let them know what their children are doing in class and encourage them to observe the seasons at home. During the Advent season, for example, recommend that they keep an Advent wreath on their family table and involve children in the prayers and lighting of the candles. You might also recommend that families use prayer booklets during special seasons, which encourage family prayer. Offer as many concrete suggestions as you can and encourage children to share with parents what they are learning in class.

A "Living" Advent Wreath

Try the following service as a way to more fully involve children in the celebration of Advent. Have six children make a circle by joining hands. Four children should stand within the circle, each carrying an unlighted candle. Three candles are purple;

one is pink. Additional children can serve as readers, pray-ers, and candle-lighters and each week of Advent these roles can be rotated.

Pray-er: O Come, O Come, Emmanuel. We wait with joy for the gift of your presence and we open our hearts to God's Word.

Reader: A reading from the letter of James (5:7–10). Be patient my friends until the Lord comes. Think of farmers who patiently wait all winter for the soil to be ready once again. You too have to be patient. Do not lose heart, because the Lord is coming soon. The Word of the Lord.

All: Thanks be to God.

Pray-er: Let us now light our Advent candle(s).

The circle opens and the candle-lighter walks through with a taper and lights the appropriate number of candles. He or she then walks out and the circle re-forms.

Let us pray. Jesus we wait for you with patience and with joy. Prepare our minds and hearts for your coming. We ask this in the name of the Father and of the Son and of the Holy Spirit.

All: Amen.

A Tree Blessing Ritual

At the beginning of Advent, explain in a note to parents that you are trying to help their children relate Christmas customs to the birth of Jesus. Ask them to help you by discussing with their children the importance of keeping Jesus in focus during all of their Christmas preparations. Suggest that one particular way they can do this is through a tree-blessing ritual at home.

Here's how you can describe it: Before you begin decorating your tree, gather around it as a family. Ask God's blessing upon it with these words: "God, our loving parent, bless this tree that will give us so much joy. Let it remind us that you have given us a great gift in Jesus. Bless us as we decorate this tree in celebration of Jesus' birth. Thank you for the gift of Christmas. Amen."

Reach Out To Others

If you have time to schedule a craft activity for Christmas, turn it into an outreach project. Instead of having children make something for parents or friends, help them focus on people who are alone and in need during the Christmas season. They can make cards for parish shut-ins, assuring them of their prayers during the Christmas liturgies. Or, they can make paper placemats for elderly parishioners to use for Christmas dinner. A message on the mats can assure the person that he or she will be remembered in prayer on Christmas day. Spend time discussing additional options

with your class. Together you might discover ways to go
beyond the class setting to reach out to those in need.

Jesus is the Reason

All of our customs relate in some way to the great gift that
God gives us in Jesus. Rather than attempt to downplay cur-
rent Christmas customs, use them to help children celebrate
Jesus as the reason for the Christmas season. We give gifts to
one another in imitation of God's gift-giving; Santa is a gift-
giver who also imitates the greatest gift-giver of all. We decorate our trees and our houses and put lights in our windows
to welcome Jesus. As children participate in traditional activities, remind them that these wonderful customs all began in
one way or another in celebration of Jesus' birth. Explain that
some people have forgotten why we do these things. Each of
us can take a role in reminding others that Jesus is the reason
for the Christmas season.

The Light of the World

Darken your teaching space and
light a votive candle. Invite children
to spend a few moments in silent
prayer, asking Jesus, the light of
the world, to guide them as they
prepare for his coming at
Christmas. You may need to do
some "quiet down" exercises the

first few times you try this. For example, ask children to breathe in God's peace and breathe out all that keeps them from it. Do this at least five times and then have them close their eyes for silent prayer. Never continue this process if there is noise or disruption.

Encourage children to ask their parents to light a candle at dinnertime throughout Advent as a reminder that Jesus is always with them.

Giving "Good Deeds"

This year, instead of having those you teach exchange gifts

for Christmas, suggest that they do "good deeds" in one another's name. They can still draw names as they ordinarily do, but explain that the "gifts" they will give one another are good deeds done in the name of the person whose name was drawn.

Possible good deeds include: doing an errand for an elderly neighbor, visiting someone who is sick or lonely, giving a gift to a needy child, writing a cheerful note to an elderly relative. The week before your gift exchange, instruct the children to write out what they have done and for whom, decorate the paper, gift wrap it, and address it to the person in the class in whose name the deeds were done. On the day of your Christmas party, invite children to share what was done in their names.

My Gift for Jesus

Here's a prayer you might want to duplicate for the children in your class. Pray it with them in your final class before Christmas and then have them decorate it and take it home to pray with their families.

Dear Jesus, I want to give you something special for your birthday, for you are my savior and the light of the world. I want to give you wonderful gifts like the Wise Men gave: gold, frankincense and myrrh. But I have nothing special to give you. And so, I will give you what I do have:

I will smile at you today by smiling at a lonely classmate. I will talk to you today by visiting my elderly neighbor. I will listen to you today by paying attention in class. I will love you today by hugging my tired parents when they get home from work. I will obey you today by doing all my chores. I offer you these simple gifts, dear Jesus, and I offer them with love. Amen.

January Activities

New Year, New Resolutions

Encourage children to do something this January to make someone else happy, some small and simple thing. Explain that giving of ourselves generously and simply is the best kind of New Year's resolution. You might want to give them suggestions written out on small slips of paper. For example: smile at five people today; offer to help your parents with dinner; pick up trash on the playground; invite a lonely child to join a game; show respect to your teachers; let someone else choose a TV program. Ask them to take the slips home and if they have done a good deed to bring the slip back to your next class. In exchange for the slip of paper, give the child a star to be placed on a special poster that reads: "Our good deeds shine like the stars in the sky."

Wait Until Epiphany

Since so many people reach out to the elderly during the weeks before Christmas, wait until after Christmas to present gift-cards to your parish shut-ins (who are not all elderly, though most are). Make special collages during the weeks of Advent by cutting up old Christmas cards and pasting them on 8x11 pieces of colored construction paper in a variety of arrangements. Then print messages on white strips and paste these at the bottom of the collages. Try to keep these messages simple, for example: "May Jesus be in your heart long after Christmas," or, "May you feel the healing touch of Jesus all year." Have the children sign their names on the back and add a personal greeting. Keep the finished cards in a special basket on your class prayer table during Advent as a reminder that we should think of others before we think of ourselves—especially during the holiday season.

Invite a member of your parish outreach committee to your first class after the holidays to receive these cards for its members who regularly visit parish shut-ins.

January Ice-Breakers

For each class in January, try an ice-breaking activity to get yourself and the children off to an enthusiastic start (after a long Christmas vacation). For example, play this (brief) winter game: invite the children to stand with you in a circle. Have the child to your right begin by saying: "What I love about

January is...." When he or she has named something, the next person takes a turn. Answers should be given as quickly as possible, so encourage the children to say whatever pops into their heads. When all have had a turn, ask the child on your left to start by saying: What I don't like about January is..." and again go around the circle quickly. You can add statements such as, "My favorite winter thing is...; I can't wait till spring because...." If you're brave, you might even throw in statements like: "What I love about this class is...; What I don't like about this class is...." Through this activity, you will learn a great deal about the children themselves and you might also learn some interesting things about your teaching.

Cheer Someone Up

In your final January class, invite children to write to the people for whom they made the collages. In the note, the children can describe one thing they have learned in religion class recently, and perhaps ask the person to pray for them as they continue to grow in the faith. As part of your closing prayer for this class, pray for the people who will receive these messages and ask for God's healing touch for them.

Winter Prayer Poems

Invite children to name all of the winter things they love and

then use these in a winter prayer-poem of four lines or so.
Give them examples like the following:

Dear God, I want you to know
just how much I love the snow.
Thank you for each beautiful flake,
and for the snowballs I can make.

If time allows, have children illustrate their prayer-poems
and take them home as a reminder of God's winter gifts.

February Activities

Service With Love

Valentine's Day is a perfect occasion for inviting those you teach to reach out in loving service to others. And, the best projects are ones that the children plan and execute themselves. You can offer information about the needs that exist in your parish community, but do allow children to choose what they will give, how they will give it, when they will give, and to whom. (If your parish has a social services ministry, perhaps you can invite in a representative to suggest alternate ways to offer service.) On Valentine's Day for example, invite your class to "adopt" someone in the parish who is sick, alone, or mentally handicapped. Offer them suggestions about ways they can reach out to this person, for example: by making Valentine cards and delivering them; by praying for this person; by making a craft for this person.

Remembering the Lonely

Try to use Valentine's Day as an opportunity to help children reach beyond their own circle of friends to remember the sick and lonely members of your parish. The week before Valentine's Day, obtain (from your parish secretary) the names and addresses of homebound, elderly, or hospitalized parishioners.

Invite the children to make Valentine cards for these people and to personalize them by writing a prayer for them on the inside. (If there are more children than names, several children can make cards for the same person.) When you finish the cards, pray together for each of the people on your list.

Ways to Grow Stronger

Giving up simple pleasures is a traditional practice of Lent. But explain to children that we don't give up things for the sake of giving them up. We do so to help ourselves grow strong in the face of difficult choices. Encourage children to "just say no" this Lent to anything that leads them away from following Jesus. Ask them to suggest ways they might do this. Remind them to begin small. Another very important lenten practice for children is to be aware of the "hurting" ones among them: those who are different, left out, made fun of, disregarded, etc. Encourage them throughout February to actively reach out to others who are sad or lonely.

Sharing Time and Attention

During Lent invite children to role-play some typical situations in which they might be called upon to share their "time" and "attention" with someone (a form of almsgiving). Place several such situations in a container and have children form groups of three. Have each group draw out one of these situations and perform it for the rest of the class. Sample situations might be as follows:

1) Two children are talking about a movie they saw. A third child approaches and tries to join the conversation. One of the first two doesn't like this intruder and is rude to him or her. The other child, however, does extend friendship.

2) A teacher is walking down the hall with a load of books as two children approach. One child suggests that they help the teacher; the other says no because the teacher was mean to him or her once. One helps the teacher and the other goes on by.

3) Two children are asked to choose a third child to do a small group project with them. The only person left, however, is an unpopular child. They want to do the project by themselves, but the teacher wants groups of three. What should they do? Leave time afterward for children to discuss how they felt about these situations.

Praying the Stations Together

During Lent take your class for a weekly visit to church for a journey along the stations of the cross. Before going into church recall that during Lent we are preparing to celebrate the greatest mysteries of our faith: Jesus' death and resurrection. Tell the children that praying the stations gives them a chance to recall Jesus' love for them. Once in church, move from station to station as a group. Briefly mention what happened at each, and then allow the children to pray silently. Keep these visits very brief so that they don't take too much time away from your regular lessons.

More on the Stations

Children can be very creative if they're given the opportunity. Suggest, for example, that they write their own stations of the cross. Research materials might include several different stations booklets, the New Testament, and their textbooks. Let each child be responsible for one station. If your group is large, have the children work in pairs. Challenge them to write each station from the perspective of one of the persons involved. For example, the first station can be written from Pilate's perspective; the second from a soldier's perspective, etc. The end result will be a collection of prayers and reflections from the people who were there—at least as your class imagines them.

Praying at Home During Lent

Prayer is one of the three traditional practices of Lent. Why not encourage the children in your class to create their own prayer space at home as a reminder to pray each day of Lent! This space can be a corner of a dresser, the top of a night stand, or even a small space on the floor of a bedroom.

Here are some items they might want to keep in this space: a crucifix or cross, one they already have or a handmade one cut from cardboard; a Bible or prayer book; and a holy card or drawing that reminds them of Jesus. If children do not have a Bible or a book of prayers, give each a typed sheet of traditional prayers to create a class lenten prayer book in this way. Ask each child to write a lenten prayer. Type all of these on one sheet to be used throughout Lent both in the classroom and at home. Also encourage children to read the Bible for a few moments before they go to bed every night during Lent.

If possible, send a note home to parents explaining what you have encouraged their children to do and encourage parents to pray and read the Bible with their children daily throughout the lenten season.

March Activities

The Cross Is Our Sign

It's very important for children to focus on the cross of Jesus during Lent because it is our primary Christian symbol. Help your class to do this in two ways: through the Sign of the Cross and by using a crucifix.

Always begin your opening class prayer as follows: "Before we pray, let us mark ourselves with a very special sign of our faith. It reminds us of the cross of Jesus, and it reminds us, too, that our God is Father and Creator, Son and Savior, Spirit and Sanctifier." Then slowly and dramatically pray: "In the name of the Father, and of the Son, and of the Holy Spirit. Amen."

Secondly, in preparation for your closing prayer, invite your class to carry a crucifix in procession to your prayer table. The leader of the procession holds the crucifix (the children can take turns being leader). Once at the prayer table, the leader turns to the others and announces: "By his cross and resurrection, Jesus Christ has set us free." All answer: "Amen." The crucifix is then reverently placed on the prayer table.

A Simple Way to Forgive

Place a container (a bowl or basket) on your prayer table and invite each child to write on a slip of paper (in private) someone he or she finds hard to forgive. Have them fold these and place them in the container. Lift this as you pray: "Dear God, before we end this class, we ask you to help us forgive those whose names are here. Forgive us, too, if we have hurt others." Afterward, discard the slips (without reading them) in the presence of the children.

Remembering the Last Supper

Have a classroom Last Supper. Bring bread (or matzo or crackers), grape juice, paper cups and napkins, and invite the children to sit in a circle on the floor. Explain to them in simple terms how Jesus took bread and blessed it, and then gave it to his friends. Pass each child a piece of bread. Next, explain how Jesus took the cup of wine, blessed it and then shared it with his friends. Pass each child a cup of grape juice. After they have shared the bread and wine with you, explain that the Last Supper was no ordinary meal, since what Jesus gave his friends was his body and blood. Tell the children that he continues to nourish us in this way in the eucharistic liturgy (Mass). While still in the circle, read to the children an account of the Last Supper from a children's Bible. Then invite them to talk to Jesus quietly in their hearts.

Sharing the Peace of Christ

In preparation for the Easter season, invite children to make a class "peace" banner. If you don't have burlap, felt, or other materials, use poster paper and paints or felt-tipped pens. Cut out large letters that read, "Peace of Christ." Allow each child to affix his or her name to the banner. Also invite each to contribute to the design. Hang the finished banner in a prominent place in your teaching space to remind the children of the importance of being peacemakers.

In your remaining classes have available small cut-out doves and each time a child does something to create a more peaceful atmosphere, add a dove to the banner near his or her name.

Preparing for Holy Week

Since many children do not attend Holy Week (Triduum) services, on your last class before Easter, set up three activity centers in your teaching space. One can be labeled Holy Thursday, one Good Friday, and the third, Easter Vigil (Holy Saturday). Divide the class into three groups and assign each group to an activity area. After fifteen minutes they can rotate and after forty-five minutes everyone should have visited every center. Here's what they do there.

At the Holy Thursday center (at which there are copies of the New Testament, index cards, and small pieces of bread) a poster gives these instructions (which can be done in any order):

•Read Matthew 26:26–30 and then go to the prayer corner to pray for a few minutes. •On an index card, write one word that describes what receiving communion means to you. Then write a two-sentence prayer thanking Jesus for this great gift. •Take a piece of the bread and eat it, remembering Jesus as you do so.

At the Good Friday center (at which there is a crucifix, 2x4 strips of purple paper (bookmark-size), and a scrolled piece of paper with Luke 23:44–49 typed on it), the poster gives these directions:

•Take the crucifix to the prayer corner and hold it reverently as you pray there for a few minutes. •On one of the purple strips, write the words "Cross of Christ" and decorate this as a bookmark in any way you wish. •Read the words on the scroll carefully, and then choose a word or phrase that strikes you and write it on the back of your purple bookmark.

At the Easter Vigil center (where there is a white candle, holy water, and copies of the baptismal promises for each child), a poster gives these directions:

•Hold the candle as you say a prayer of thanks to God for your baptism. Ask God to make you a strong Christian. •Bless yourself with the holy water, slowly and reverently. Then go to the prayer corner for a few minutes of silent prayer. •Read the baptismal promises slowly. Circle the one that is easiest for you. Underline the one that is most difficult. On the opposite side of the paper, write a prayer asking for God's help to live these promises.

Of course, do encourage children to attend the Triduum liturgies with their families.

April Activities

Getting to Know "Grace"

Children understand that each of the sacraments has signs or symbols that we can see, and they understand that Jesus gave us these symbolic actions, either directly or indirectly, but they stumble when it comes to the concept of grace. Grace is a word that is no longer used on a regular basis even in church settings, and it means "gift from God." Each of the sacraments bestows the gift of God's own life.

To get this point across, invite children to do the following exercise: Give each child a tiny seed from a packet of marigold seeds. Ask them to examine them closely. Do they look like flowers? Do they have life? Do they have potential for life?

Most acknowledge that though the seeds don't look like flowers, they can become flowers when they are planted and cared for. Explain that God dwells in us in a way we can't see and that God's presence is nourished by the sacraments and prayer, just as a seed is nourished by the sun and water. Just

as it takes faith to believe that a seed can become a flower, so it takes faith to believe that God's grace is given to us to help us reach our full potential.

Invite the children to plant their seeds at home—where most—if cared for properly—will eventually produce flowers!

Easter Reminders

Read the entire text from Matthew, chapter 25, verses 31–46. Discuss as a class what this means on a day-to-day basis. How might children reach out to others in very practical ways, beginning today? As a reminder you might want to give each child a cut-out brightly colored flower with these words printed on it: "Remember that Jesus needs you this day." Encourage children to keep these at home in a visible place throughout the Easter season.

Remember that Jesus needs you this day.

The Easter Season

In this activity children search for the true meaning of Easter. This can be done even after Easter Sunday, since the Easter season lasts for fifty days. Write out or type the fol-

lowing ten sentences, adapted from Luke, Chapter 24:
1) Very early on Sunday morning, the women came to the tomb. 2) They went in, but they didn't find the body of Jesus. 3) Two messengers stood before them in shining clothes. 4) The women were frightened but the messengers said this to them: 5) Why are you looking here for a living person? 6) This is a place for dead people. 7) Jesus is not here. 8) He has risen from the dead. 9) The women left the tomb and went to the apostles and the other followers. 10) The women told them everything that had happened at the tomb.

Cut these sentences into strips and place each one in a colored plastic egg. Hide the eggs, outside if possible. After all the eggs are located, let the class put the hidden message in its proper order. Then read Luke 24:1–13.

We Are Lights for Jesus

Place a children's Bible and a candle on a special table in your class. Explain to the children that the Bible is God's Word, which is read to us each Saturday or Sunday at Mass. Tell the children: If we listen to God's Word and follow it, we grow as children of God. Prayerfully read to the children the story of the loaves and the fishes. Allow them to ask questions and to comment on the story. Now light the candle.

Explain that each of us received candles at baptism to remind us that we are "the light of the world." Invite each child to come forward, and placing one hand on the Bible, to pray, either silently or aloud, a prayer of thanks to Jesus for all the ways in which he nourishes and strengthens them.

Using Easter Symbols

Easter is our most significant liturgical feast but children rarely recognize it as such because most preparations center on candy, eggs, and baskets. Each year try to focus on one Easter symbol that emphasizes the religious message that Jesus is risen from the dead. Some symbols you can use are: light (Paschal Candle), special words (alleluia, rejoice, resurrection), water (as the baptismal sign), an empty cross, and spring flowers.

Begin talking about one particular symbol a few weeks before Easter. If, for example, the symbol is light, ask the children to discuss all the ways they can think of that we use light. Then ask them to write about or verbally describe how they feel in total darkness and then how they feel when a light is turned on.

During the class before Easter spend some time making a visible reminder. Again, using the symbol of light, give the children copies of a large Paschal Candle. They can color the candle, cut it out, and mount it with glue on a piece of construction paper. Somewhere on the construction paper they can write the words: "Jesus our Light is risen!" They can then tape a small piece of yarn on the back-side of the pictures so they can be hung in their rooms at home.

A Message for Easter

Here's a simple activity that reminds children of the true message of Easter Sunday. For it you will need a plastic colored egg for each child. Type the following prayer/poem and fold it up inside each egg. On your last class before Easter Sunday, distribute the eggs and tell children to open them on Easter Sunday morning to receive a special message from you. Here's the message:

Here is a present just for you, a symbol of Easter and new life, too. For here's what happened on Easter Day: Jesus was raised from the tomb where he lay! So Easter eggs are not just for fun. They remind us that Jesus is God's own Son. So when you eat an egg on Easter Day, Remember Jesus—and here's what to say: "Thank you, Jesus, for sharing your love, Thank you for all God's gifts from above."

A Child's Prayer for Easter

Here's a prayer that you might want to use with your class during the Easter season. Have a different child read each line and at the end everyone can pray "Alleluia, Amen!"

> Dear Jesus, Risen Savior,
>
> thank you for this Easter Day.
>
> I am so happy that you are risen from the dead
>
> and that you now live in my heart,forever and ever.
>
> You have shown me, Jesus, how to trust in God
>
> who takes care of me and guides me in all things.
>
> Your resurrection tells me that God is always with me,
>
> giving me new life, new faith, new hope, and new love.
>
> Happy Easter, dear Jesus!
>
> May I always be a sign to others
>
> of your Easter joy and peace.
>
> Alleluia, Amen!

May Activities

A May Celebration

For one of your May sessions, invite those you teach to bring to class spring flowers. Those who don't have flowers growing at home can bring in drawings of flowers or handmade paper ones. Together decorate your class prayer table with these offerings. Then pray spontaneous prayers together, thanking God first of all for the gift of flowers. Then encourage the children to pray prayers of thanks for any gifts of new life that springtime brings. At a second May session you might want to plan together a thanksgiving May procession to honor Mary, but also to focus on God's springtime gifts. Invite the children to decide what to carry in the procession, which songs to sing, and which prayers to say. End this class with the actual procession, which the children will enjoy all the more because they have prepared it.

Remembering Mary

Plan to have a class May procession. Since many parishes no longer hold such processions, some children may never have heard of this custom. Explain that walking in procession toward a certain point makes the event more solemn. Also, the walking allows participants to sing and pray together. Plan a procession route with your class and allow them to choose the songs and prayers. The procession can start where your class meets and return there, where a statue or picture of Mary has a place of honor. Invite the children to bring fresh flowers to be placed in a vase near the statue or picture, at the end of the procession.

A Forget-Me-Not Activity

Toward the end of the teaching year, when classes are winding down, is a good time to help children think of ways to remember over the summer what they have learned. You can, of course, prepare a list of "things to remember" for them and distribute this at your last class. To make the items more appealing, however, try this: Draw some large flowers on pieces of construction paper (two flowers per sheet), and cut these out. (Make at least 20 flowers at first.) On the front side of each flower write a question. On the back, write the answer. During your last few classes, play "pick a flower" with the children. Allow them to take turns choosing a flower. If they can answer the question completely, let them keep the flower. You may end up making a lot of flowers, but if each one represents something learned and remembered, it's worth the time and effort. Try putting prayers on some of the flowers, too. When the children know the prayer by heart, the flower goes home with them.

End-of-year Prayer

Sometime before your final class of the year, ask each of the children to write a one-line petition that requests God's help over the summer. Then put all of these together into one prayer that you duplicate and give each child to pray every day until religion classes begin again. Here's a sample class prayer:

> Dear God,
>
> Keep us safe this summer. Protect us from danger as we play. Help us to be kind to everyone we meet, and to say thank you for your summer gifts like sun and water and sand, and for trips to new places. Help us to understand all that we learned about you this summer and to pray every day of the summer. Please don't let us get sunburned. Amen.

A Pot-luck Celebration

If your class is one that will be receiving a sacrament this year, arrange for your own class pot-luck celebration. Students can send invitations to family members and even plan a simple prayer service to be held before the meal. If your class is small you might want to have this celebration in your home or the home of one of the students. If you have a large class, the celebration might be held in the church hall. If this kind of get-together is not possible, at least plan to send a personal note of congratulations to each child receiving the sacrament. If possible mail these notes rather than just handing them out. Receiving personal mail at home is a significant happening for most children, and it will highlight the importance of this sacramental moment in their lives.

"Catching the Spirit"

Because the feast of Pentecost is celebrated after our classes are over, try to do several activities throughout the year that focus on the Holy Spirit, especially an activity called "Catch the Spirit." Set aside ten minutes of class to read the children several verses from Scripture and challenge them to listen for mention of the Holy Spirit. Anyone who hears such a reference, is invited to yell out "Holy Spirit." Each time a child yells these words, everyone should stand up and recite the "Glory Be...." Then go on with the reading until the next reference is discovered.

At first the children may not listen to the Scripture readings because they are only listening for references to the Holy Spirit. But after one or two times they listen very intently and are able to repeat what was read.

Answering as a Team

As your teaching year draws to a close, spend time reviewing what you have covered. Choose words, facts, and definitions from your lessons, and ask the children to form two teams. Pose a question and give Team One time to deliberate and give a group answer. If correct, they gain a point. If incorrect, Team Two gets to suggest an answer. Reviewing in this way calls for group answers, and thus no one is left out.

All-Year-Long Activities

Time for Review

Though we should not equate faith with knowledge of the faith, we do a disservice as catechists if we don't expect children to remember what we are teaching. Try to encourage this kind of learning through brief review games before each class. For example, write out ten or so questions based on your previous lesson and quiz the children in various ways. Sometimes have a knowledge "bee," sometimes a written quiz, sometimes a Jeopardy-type quiz in which you give the answers and the children form the questions.

Doing the Right Thing

Make a sign for your teaching space (with children's help) that says, "Do the Right Thing!" Ask the children what they think this means in practical terms. Have one child record everyone's suggestions on slips of paper. Have a few suggestions of your own written on slips, for example: help your parents; respect your teachers; be polite to everyone; be kind to classmates (especially those who are left out); keep your room neat; do your homework carefully. Before the children leave, have each choose one slip and encourage them to try throughout the week to practice what is on it.

Sharing Bible Stories

If you have a children's Bible, read the children stories from it in each class session, from your first class on. If you don't have one, tell some New Testament stories in your own words from the Bible. Some stories that particularly appeal to children are: the Multiplication of the Loaves and Fishes (Matt. 14:13–21), the Raising of Jarius' Daughter (Luke 8:40–56), the Last Supper (Mark 14:22–26), Jesus Feeds His Friends (John 21:1–13), and Jesus Meets Two Friends on the Road to Emmaus (Luke 24:13–35). After the telling (or reading) of the story, have children respond by writing a note to Jesus saying how they feel about what he did and said. Have them place these letters on your prayer table in a special container as a sign that they are followers of Jesus.

Teaching about Marriage

Though most of our children will one day marry in the church, very few know much about the marriage rite. To correct this, use the following activity for junior-high classes. (You will need at least two sessions for this.) Divide the class into pairs, not necessarily boy/girl pairs, though if evenly matched, this works best. Explain that they have been asked to prepare the wedding ceremony for a couple about to marry and that they are to choose among options for the gathering and entrance rites, the Scripture readings, the rite for the exchange of vows, the rite for the blessing of rings, the prayers during the Liturgy of the Eucharist, and the concluding rites. Also ask them to prepare the general intercessions and to choose the music.

Because participants could never make choices without guidelines, have available for their use several copies of *Celebrating Marriage: Preparing the Wedding Liturgy* (published by Oregon Catholic Press, 5536 NE Hassalo, Portland, OR 97213).

Sacrament Spelling Bee

While it may be true that it's more important for children to understand the sacraments than to spell them, it doesn't hurt if they can spell them, too. Give each child in your class a list of the seven sacraments—misspelled. Have them look up the correct spelling in their textbooks and write it next to the misspelled word. Next, have partners quiz each other over and over until each can spell every word correctly. Finally, have a spelling bee—with holy cards for the winner. It's not at all unusual that every child ends up spelling every sacrament correctly, so you might want to have a holy card for everyone.

Once the spelling is mastered, you might want to have a "definition" bee.

Remembering Baptism

Ask the children to bring to class some remembrance of their baptism: a candle, baptismal certificate, white garments, or pictures. Since children will tend to forget, you might send a letter home with them the week before, requesting these items. Let the children take turns describing to the rest of the class something about the objects they have brought in and what they think the objects mean. After these presentations, role-play a baptism ceremony, using some of the objects belonging to the children.

Let them take turns being priest, infant, parents, godparents, and congregation.

Fun with Sacrament Names

I've heard people over the years say that the names of the sacraments, and other church words for that matter, are too difficult for children to remember. But think about it. They can remember Rumpelstiltskin and Tyrannosaurus Rex! And they can remember church words as well. Repetition is the key as with any other learning. Here's a simple way to help those you teach to learn and remember the names of the sacraments.

First print the sacrament names on a poster. Then print each one in large letters on index cards (with lots of space between each letter) and cut out the letters and place them in an envelope (seven envelopes for the seven sacraments).

Give the envelopes out at random and challenge the children (working in groups of two or three) to put the letters together in the right order. They can find the correct spelling on the poster. Once they are able to do this successfully, remove the poster and redistribute the envelopes (at random). The first group that puts the letters in the correct order wins. After doing this several times, the children know the names of the sacraments and can spell them correctly as well.

Books by Gwen Costello

Junior High Prayer Services by Themes

These twenty-one prayer services for students (grades 6–8) can be used as opening or closing prayers for regular classes or during retreats. They will invite junior high students to be comfortable with themselves, to reflect on their attitudes, and to respond to their Christian class to follow Jesus.

88 pages, $12.95 (order J-67)

Praying with the Saints
30 Classroom Services for Children

Each of these thirty creative, easy-to-use prayer services and activities focuses on an aspect of a saint's life that children (ages 7–12) can imitate. Includes a mini-biography of each saint, ideas for prayer, an action response, and an optional activity. 104 pages, $12.95 (order J-30)

Classroom Prayer Services for the Days of Advent and Lent

Looking for more meaningful ways to celebrate the seasons? These sixty creative services involve children (ages 7–12) in celebrating God's presence through processions, veneration of the Bible, prayer patterns, speaking parts, guided meditations, and blessings. Catholic customs such as praying to Mary and the saints, practicing virtue, and fasting and abstinence are also presented. Easily incorporated into Advent and Lent lesson plans.

144 pages, $12.95 (order B-39)

Seven Steps to Great Religion Classes
Gwen Costello and Joe Paprocki

The authors take you step by step through seven important elements of a "great religion class": the qualities of a good catechist; the process of lesson planning; skills needed to create a positive environment; strategies for motivating children; techniques for maintaining and handling discipline; and skills in sharing and leading meaningful prayer experiences. Each chapter includes reflection and discussion questions, and a concluding prayer. A must-have for every catechist and religion teacher!

80 pages, $7.95 (order C-09)

Available at religious bookstores or from:

TWENTY-THIRD PUBLICATIONS

PO BOX 180 · 185 WILLOW STREET (P) MYSTIC, CT 06355 · 1-800-321-0411
FAX: 1-800-572-0788 BAYARD E-MAIL: ttpubs@aol.com

Call for a free catalog